Our
Voices,
Our
Land

Our Voices, Our Land

Words by
the Indian Peoples of the Southwest

Photographs by
Stephen Trimble and Harvey Lloyd

Based on an Audio-visual Show Created
for The Heard Museum, Phoenix, Arizona

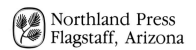 Northland Press
Flagstaff, Arizona

Edited by Stephen Trimble

FIRST EDITION
ISBN 0-87358-412-0 softcover
ISBN 0-87358-427-9 hardcover
Library of Congress Catalog Card Number 86-61159
Composed in the United States of America
Printed in Japan by Toppan Printing Company

Library of Congress Cataloging in Publication Data

Our voices, our land.

    1. Indians of North America—Southwest, New—Exhibitions.
2. Heard Museum of Anthropology and Primitive Art—Exhibi-
tions. I. Trimble, Stephen A. II. Lloyd, Harvey. III. Heard
Museum of Anthropology and Primitive Art.
E78.S7087   1986   929'.00497   86-61159
ISBN 0-87358-412-0 (pbk.)
ISBN 0-87358-427-9 (cloth)

Royalties from this publication will be shared with The Heard
Museum's Roger A. Lyon Endowment Fund for Native American
Research, Education, and Professional Development, as recipient
for the Indian people whose words appear in this book.

PHOTOGRAPHS:

cover: feast day, San Juan Pueblo, New Mexico   ST
i & iii: Monument Valley, Arizona   HL
frontispiece: petroglyphs, Spirit Mountain, Nevada,
    emergence place of the Yuman peoples   ST
viii: war captain, Tesuque Pueblo feast day, New Mexico   ST
back cover: Monument Valley, Arizona   HL

Contents

The debut of "Our Voices, Our Land" propelled The Heard Museum into a new and innovative role, that of communicator. This thirty-minute, continuously running, multi-screen, multi-media production serves as an introduction to the museum's new permanent exhibit, "Native Peoples of the Southwest," and was a daring venture for the institution. We wondered if museum visitors would be truly captured by the intimate, yet involving setting of the gallery-theater and by the voices of the native peoples, the spiritual music composed by R. Carlos Nakai, and the depth of imagery presented in the panoramic landscapes and powerful portraits of the people themselves.

The answer is a resounding "Yes!" In every way, the production meets our dream; provocative and sensitive, "Our Voices, Our Land" is a show stopper.

The Heard Museum thanks its many native American friends who articulated their feelings about themselves, their families, and their cultural heritages. To Image Makers, Inc., of New York City, Harvey Lloyd, Executive Producer–Director; Stephen Trimble, Sound Recorder and Photographer; and Bonnie Durrance, Producer–Associate Director, we acknowledge our appreciation of their professional talent in developing this true, dramatic, and poignant show.

We are equally indebted to the corporate underwriter of the audio-visual program, American Continental Corporation, who believed in the importance of the message and in its potential impact on the audience.

This magnificent book also reflects the love, dedication, and professionalism of our former Deputy Director/Chief Curator, Dr. Robert G. Breunig; Museum Exhibit Designer, Patrick M. Neary; and Ralph Appelbaum Associates, Inc., of New York City, and their devotion to the development of all the creative components of the exhibition, "Native Peoples of the Southwest." And, most especially, I wish to mark the support of The Heard Museum Board of Trustees and my staff, whose support was the bedrock of the project.

We hope that the following pages provide the reader with the same impressions and respect that viewers gain from their visit to The Heard Museum, Phoenix, Arizona.

MICHAEL J. FOX, *Director*

Foreword

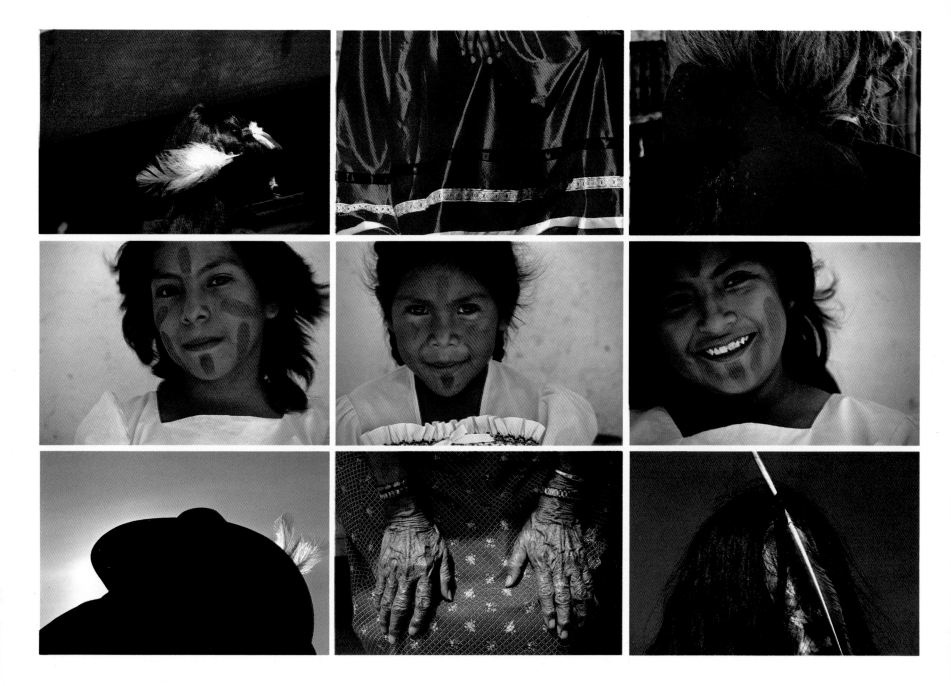

Writer Barry Lopez once told me what an old Eskimo man said to him when he first went to the Arctic: "When you come into a new country, listen a lot."

I listened a lot.

This book grew from an assignment that allowed me the privilege of listening. It grew from the audio-visual program "Our Voices, Our Land" at The Heard Museum in Phoenix, Arizona. The show introduces the wing that houses "Native Peoples of the Southwest," the permanent collection of the museum.

My field assignment from the Heard and from the show's director, Harvey Lloyd, was to record the voices for the soundtrack of the audio-visual program and to photograph landscape and people. Harvey photographed the three-screen panoramic landscapes that appear here as triptychs. With the guidance of museum curator Dr. Robert Breunig, we developed an outline based on seven themes, and in May 1984, began traveling the Southwest, trying to reach all the tribes in Arizona and northern New Mexico in one summer. The scope was ambitious: Rio Grande Pueblos, Acoma, Zuni, Hopi,

Navajo, Hualapai, Havasupai, Yavapai, Apache, Pima, Papago, Yaqui, Maricopa, Quechan, Cocopah, Chemehuevi, Mojave. But we had an absolute deadline: the show must be running by late October. And so we began.

From the beginning, Bob Breunig knew what he wanted to hear: the spirit of the show must bring to life Southwest Indian people and communicate their vitality. Bob had involved native Americans as consultants throughout the exhibit, and his dream for "Our Voices, Our Land" was to have no narration written by Anglo anthropologists or writers, only the voices of the Indian people, who would speak for themselves. In this way, we hoped the show would make vivid the *people,* inspiring museum visitors who would then view the exhibit cases full of artifacts with the voices of contemporary Indian people ringing in their ears.

To find these voices, I contacted people I knew from having lived in the Southwest all my life, people suggested by the staff of the Heard, and friends of friends. It helped that The Heard Museum has an excellent reputation on the reservations; the Indians trusted the Heard—as much as they trust any white man's museum.

Introduction

The response of the Indian people was astounding. All of the quotes in this book come from these 1984 recordings. Virtually everyone I talked with understood immediately and intuitively what we had in mind; in fact, they understood better than we did. I tried to encourage people to talk, and to keep them talking. I did my very best to be a receptive, respectful sponge.

I listened.

With the understanding of the Indian people, their trust in the Heard, and their willingness to accept me, many times I would find myself deep into a recording session within a half-hour of meeting someone. Often, one of the Indian people and I would laugh when he or she would realize what was happening, abruptly stop, and say: "Tell me again what are you going to do with this tape." I could imagine them saying to themselves: "Who is this man? Why am I saying these intimate things? Can this situation be trusted?"

I also photographed the people I interviewed. I bartered: permission to use portraits in our slide show in return for the prints I promised to send them. When someone gave me their address, I asked them to write it on a model release form. It seemed to leave everyone with the agreeable feeling that they had participated in a fair trade.

Most people on the reservations have no phones. To reach them, I went to their homes. Because I was trying to cover so much ground so quickly, I moved fast and tried to avoid time wasted by waiting. Some people talked with me on first meeting. Others made appointments for that day or the next—and kept them. Others said to return in a week, knowing that might mean several hundred miles of driving. When I *did* come back, they nearly always relented.

I visited a Papago saguaro camp. I spent a day with a Navajo family, walking along with my cameras as they took their sheep out to graze. In June, I stumbled by chance on a Pima feast day at the little church in Sacaton, Arizona. The entertainment consisted of alternate rounds of traditional basket dancers with face paint, *matachines,* chicken scratch (border polka music), and break-dance demonstrations by the teenage boys. Perhaps a hundred and fifty Pimas were there, and two whites: a man married to a Pima, and myself.

I watched until I felt comfortable and until I guessed that everyone had sufficient time to look me over. Then I asked the master of ceremonies (who was raffling off cakes and such) to announce that there was a photographer present who would take free portraits of anyone interested. That invitation was accepted by twenty-five people.

Early in the summer, a Papago man met me at The Heard Museum one morning for an interview. I was nervous. I had done no location recording or interviewing before the beginning of this project, and my taping had not been yielding technically adequate recordings. I was eager to have this interview go well.

I delivered my standard introductory speech while setting up equipment. He remained completely impassive, however, his face a mask of unresponsive neutrality. I floundered, searching for the right approach to engage him, but it was difficult to even maintain eye contact. He watched for about ten minutes, then smiled and said, "Are you nervous?"

I said yes, indeed, I was. And the ice broke. He said how silly I seemed, my eyes darting every which way. Finally, I relaxed and he began to talk—eloquently and easily.

Some of the most moving speakers came from the Hualapai Reservation in Peach Springs, Arizona. The woman who administers their bilingual education program offered to set up interviews with a wide range of people in the tribe, and I promised to pay a token twelve dollars per hour for their time.

I gave her a week's warning before my visit, and she scheduled me hour by hour for two days—with everyone from the tribal chairman to the parole officer to the elders.

One man was convinced I was an anthropologist ready to record his life history. When I turned on the recorder, he hunkered down, put his fingers to his brow, closed his eyes, and talked. In a monotone, almost without pause, he started with his grandfather's hunting stories and ended with his own heart surgery. His "life story," although paramount to him, was almost useless to us; the cadence was all wrong (I admit to nodding off to sleep during his two-hour monologue).

But when finally finished, he responded to my questions with great feeling. His voice opens our show.

The Hualapai tribal chairman, on the other hand, began by stiffly reading his campaign literature verbatim into the microphone. But gradually he eased back in his chair and began to talk sadly about the problems of a small tribe with no economic base. He ended with a remarkable phrase: if the Hualapai people did not develop some way of making money from their reservation, "then there is no justification for our existence" as a reservation, as a tribe.

I went to see one of the elders, a woman in her eighties. My knock on the door of the Bureau of Indian Affairs crackerbox house roused an elderly woman. She shuffled to the screen door and peered out over the closed lower window at me. I saw her only from the eyes up—eyes that were tired and properly suspicious of a strange white man at her door, eyes that were yet deep and clear.

She was expecting me, and asked me in.

Many anthropologists had interviewed her and the recording equipment did not bother her. This woman was a storyteller—the past and the present blended in her memory. The stories told her by her grandmother about *her* grandmother were as real as the gray pattern in the formica of her kitchen table.

I would ask a question, and she would tell a story. She told me of the forced march of the Hualapais in the 1870s, when the United States soldiers beat to death her great-great grandfather because he could not walk fast enough in the heat. She told it through the eyes of her grandmother, but as she told the story, she was there herself: "I see these things still in my own eyes yet; when, when will I ever forget?"

She told of being forced to attend a Bureau of Indian Affairs boarding school when she was a child, of being beaten by the white matrons for speaking Hualapai. The teachers told her: "Forget your Indian foods, forget the names of the mountains and the rivers, and above all, forget your language. Just speak English."

She cried when she talked. I was too moved to cry. Her eloquence eclipsed her aging face, her appearance, her house.

Her voice and her stories ring out from our soundtrack ten times a day at the museum.

A Hopi man, an elder, helped construct a corn storage room for the museum exhibit. One night, he agreed to talk with me; we sat in his

motel room in the heart of urban Phoenix, and he spoke the way he must speak to apprentices in kivas. He talked about what it means to be Hopi, about the gifts of the creator, about the lack of true traditionalists, about Hopi prophecies. He talked directly at a subject for a while; then he would pause, back up, and talk at it from the side; then circle it and talk at it from behind. The repetition was ritualistic. I thought how even more profound he would sound in Hopi, in a kiva.

I recorded an Apache sculptor in his studio. I talked with shy Pima women in an Arizona State University classroom where they were taking classes in bilingual eduction. I recorded Hopi families in their homes, an Apache medicine man in a cross-cultural-studies institute, a Navajo man in the auditorium of a county arts center, a

Papago poet in her office at the University of Arizona (pausing when her neighboring professor began pounding on his typewriter).

At Santa Fe's Indian Market, a huge weekend gathering of native American artists from all over the Southwest, I reserved a conference room at the Fine Arts Museum and wrangled people away from their booths for a half-hour at a time. A young Jemez Pueblo woman spoke about the feelings she put into her prize-winning sculpture: "First, we are artists." A sensitive Navajo weaver cried when she spoke of her grandmother's advice: "Without your family, you are nothing." Her words, which end our section on "Family," hang in the air while the face of a little Hualapai girl dissolves slowly from the screen.

I spent two days photographing a Whiteriver Apache girl's puberty ceremony, watching the whole community dance her into womanhood. I photographed a Hualapai mourning ceremony, where the people cry for their dead of the previous year for a day and a night under a brush shade (ramada), then burn the ramada at dawn.

Each person and experience took its place on an internal map, a piece of reality connected to every other by my path and our program: An eloquent Apache artist who lived on the Pima reservation and who spoke to me over the clink of dishes in a restaurant along the Interstate; a Navajo family in an isolated hogan on the rim of a mesa above Monument Valley in Utah; the old Hualapai woman in Peach Springs; the potters in the pueblos near my home in New Mexico.

I felt like a runner, dashing back and forth between these cross-points in the web, carrying words and photographs—gathering the gifts shared by generous people, and taking them down the strand of highway to the museum through the insane traffic (and 113° summer heat) of downtown Phoenix.

The Heard was the center of the web, where eventually the show would run, where Navajo/Ute flute-player R. Carlos Nakai composed the music. To the first few images and stories we could share with him, and to the outline, Carlos added his entire heritage and his feeling for the solitude of canyons and mesas. I hummed his music when I returned to the road.

The land gave remarkable things to me, as did the people. In many cases, I would have only one chance to photograph, and time after time, something wonderful would happen with light or with animals or with storms. Burrowing owls fluttered around the crosses in a Papago cemetery. A red-tailed hawk perched on a saguaro, backlighting making its feathers and the saguaro spines a hot golden haze of light. Purple mist hung behind the San Francisco Peaks, lightning bolts shooting from black clouds above.

My field trips added up to some forty-five

hours of taping, two hundred and seventy-five rolls of pictures, and endless miles in my truck. We also used pictures from my files, covering some twelve years of wandering the Southwest.

On the day we blessed the completed exhibit, I stood in the museum listening to Navajo and Apache medicine men tell their ancestors that we had treated their belongings with respect. Apache and Pima drummers beat purifying vibrations through the exhibit, vibrations that seemed to enter each of our bodies and pulse outward from a resting place in our breastbones.

I looked at the map of this land. I could feel the strands of the web overlying the map and vibrating with the drums. The beat traveled outward to everyone who had given us their words, their clear-eyed portrait, their feeling for the land. They all understood. They might never see the exhibit or this book, but they had shared their words and their lives and their souls with all of us.

I had traveled the strands of the web with my truck and my dog, my cameras and tape recorder, gathering feelings, slides, tapes, and transcripts and passing them on to Bonnie Durrance in Washington, D.C.—a far-flung, pivotal intersection in the web. Bonnie produced, edited and designed the show; she created a coherent and powerful distillation from the packages that I sent to her from places like Globe, and Grants, and Kingman, from Harvey Lloyd's landscapes, and from R. Carlos Nakai's music. Her vision of the show formed the basis for this book.

Everyone understood what they were about—from the land and the people to the computer programmer. Each footfall on the path that began with storytellers in Peach Springs and sunrises over sacred mountains was placed in a line directed at communicating what we had learned.

I made many new friends. And I learned about ritual. I try now to pay more attention to the earth, to always note such easily taken-for-granted miracles as sunrises and moonsets. I park my truck at night so that my camper faces east and the sun shines directly in the back door every morning. My feeling for the Southwest has a new layer of understanding. The spirit of the Indian people is entwined with the land.

It always will be.

STEPHEN TRIMBLE

For the young
Indian people of the Southwest
May you find
a smooth path between two worlds

The Land

The land, the hills, and the mountain has a life in it.
The ground which we stand on has a life in it.

All the nations call the Earth
as Mother Nature.

At the beginning, the Hualapais and Mojaves heard the flood was coming. And one of the elderly people hollowed out a log and put his daughter in it and told her that this big flood was coming and she should stay in there until she knows it's going to be dry. When the flood came, the log got caught up on that high peak and stayed there until the land all dried.

When she got out, everybody was gone.
There were two gods there; one was called the good one and
one was the evil one. The good one told her to try to survive.
She lived there for a long time, until she conceived.
Eventually they multiplied. Each people went to different places
and this is how they got their names.

The old people told us
to respect the land,
they tell you to take care of it,
take care of it and in turn
it will take care of you.

18   THE LAND

Our power comes from the earth.

The land means a lot to us.
It means home.
It's so dry, no water—
but it's home to us.

I belong to this place.

I feel very close to the moon. I feel close to the sun.
I feel close to the earth, the femininity of Mother Earth.
When you think about all these things, you just become
a part of them and they become a part of you.

You go out and get a certain piece of rock. It's not just a rock.
It's got energy forces in it, it's a living thing, too.

You look at that mountain, that mountain has a spirit,
that mountain has holiness. There's a quiet there and yet
there's a fervor there. And if you've ever seen clouds there
you see that mountain like a hand grasping those clouds.

There's life up there. That's why it's sacred.

Sustenance

Here, we need the rain. That's where our prayers are going.
That's why we have dances.

In our childhood days,
in the evenings about four o'clock,
you would hear the faint sounds
of thunder from somewhere else,
and you finally notice that it's
drizzling out there, and when you
wake up in the morning,
it's still drizzling.
Soaking into the ground slowly.

It's because they were living
traditionally.

What do I see in the desert?
I see a peaceful air,
the smell of the greasewood,
the yellow flowers
on the ironwood trees,
the sunsets.
I miss the animals—you always
hear the quail and the doves
in the morning.
And the heat itself
is so soothing to the body.

I like pines, but they're not mine.

My grandma's husband went to Supai on horseback and he bring
peach tree and fig trees, and we used to have a lot of peaches.
We have lots to eat down there. Melons, and corn . . .

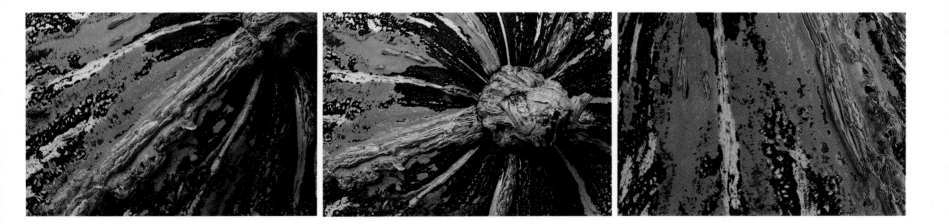

Corn is the center of life, the essence of life.

I still have a field. I still plant my corn.
Because why should I participate and pray for rain
if I don't have any plants for the rains to come and nourish?

We used to grind it on the rock and on Saturday and Sunday,
that's all we did, was grind corn.
You grind corn Friday night for yourself.
Saturday you grind for your aunt.
Sunday you grind for whoever you think *needs* cornmeal.

Before you go hunting, the important thing is that you are going to have a little prayer . . . to the Mother Nature, the nature of the sky, and then the animal, and then you more or less cry a little bit, and ask Mother Nature to spare you some meat.

When you went into that forest, you had to *be* that deer.

Eat what the birds eat, they tell us.
The birds, they know.

When you go out gathering food, we have to send a gladness, a prayer, that these things are on the fields, just being planted by our Creator.

We must try and worship the land, the ground and the stars
and the skies, for they are the ones that have spirit.
They are the mighty spirits
which guides and direct us,
which help us to survive.

Family

A lot of the culture comes from the family.

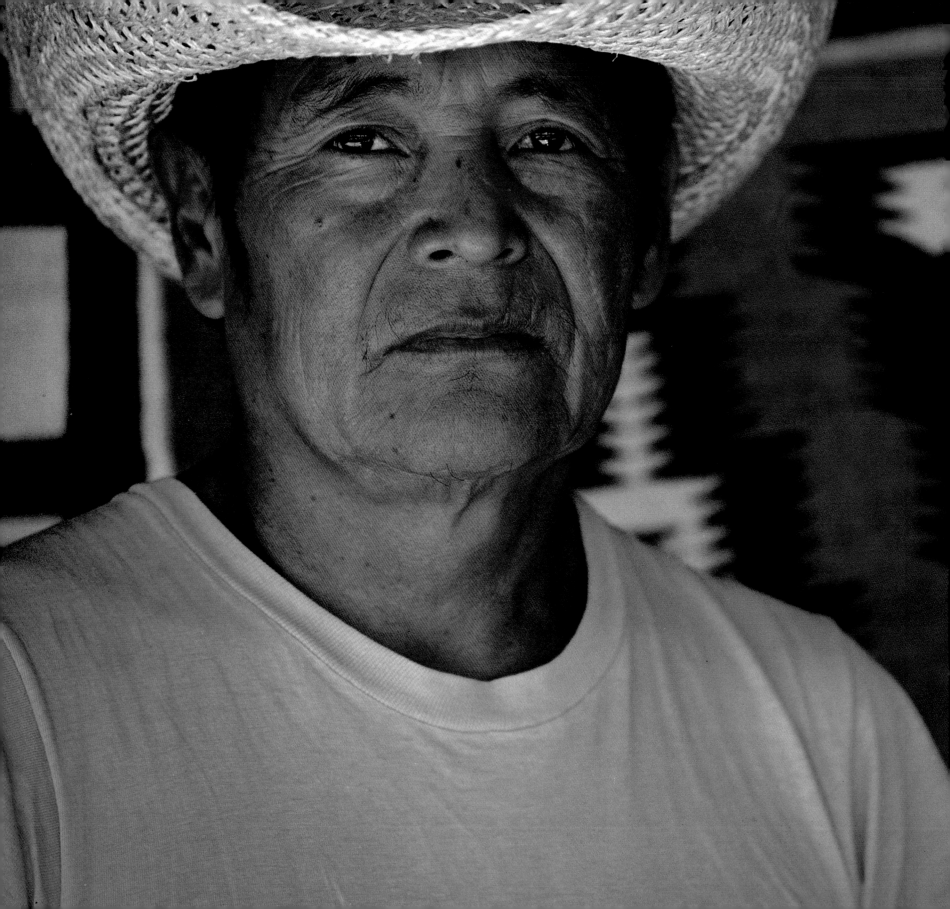

We still try to perpetuate those roles.
And I, for instance, try to perpetuate that role of my clan,
The Clan Who Walks Around You,
who's on the outside of the camp to protect my family.
I carry forth and perpetuate that role I would have had traditionally
in that I'm still a warrior.
I'm a warrior in the sense that I advocate for my people
and speak on behalf of my people.

The womanfolks know their place. It's at the home.
Being a mother.

In Apache, they just become a woman right away.
The whole family had to get involved in it.
They say that the abalone shell that she has on her forehead
represent the giant abalone shell that the first Apache woman
was inside of during the flash flood.

She run toward the sun four times.
Everything in Apache is four times.
Four different directions. . .
The people that follow her
in Apache say, "May she run fast."
This four days is the most important part of her life.

After the Hopi girl changes into maturity, they take a little piece
of hair down the side by your ear and cut it.
That shows that you have changed into maturity.
At the wedding ceremony, when all the aunts come in and
everybody, every one of them, touches the bride's hair, then
they tie the man's and the woman's hair together to join them.

I really disappointed my mother
when I married into another tribe.
But I was listening to my brother
and he said, "You have your own
life to live, you have to do what
you think is best for you."
In later years, she said to me,
"he doesn't speak the same
language as I do so if he got mad
at me he can say it in Indian so I
don't know what he is saying."
And she said, "I love him."

You water your children like you water the tree.

One thing Grandma taught was that
without your family
you were nothing.
She taught me to be there for *all*
my family. And it's not very easy
these days to teach that to people
who are younger than you.
I do not know whether my older
daughter will be there for me
when I need her, as I am there
for my mother now.

Families are very important.
There would not be so many
people lost and wandering if
families were all there
for one another.

Community

The Hualapai lived in bands. Each one had a leader.
When the Hualapais were being rounded up, the ones
that weren't able to escape and go down into the canyons,
they were the ones that were captured and
forced into the march down to La Paz.

La Paz is way down below Parker.
They throw them in no man's land. Just sand.
It was so hot, many of them died.
My grandfather was whipped to death!
Oh, I see these things still in my own eyes yet.
When, when will I ever forget?

I feel a little bit lost.

When I want to find my identity, I usually have to go to

that little museum, and I'll look back

and see this is the way it was when my parents were younger.

You look back at these old photographs

and you see them when they were children

and they were living in these real light homes—

it looked like a wind could come along and blow it away.

Some people even lived in caves.

Those were the old type of
traditional buildings. They are much
smaller, might be little more than
six feet high to the ceilings.
Of course, they built them
connecting together
and right on top of one another,
maybe two–three stories high.
In my childhood days, you have
woven blankets made out of wool,
and you have a bedding that
you would lay down on the floor.
It would be a sheep skin.

There is so much incredible goodness that comes out of
the pueblos and out of the people.
It exists there, in those villages, a hundred times more so
than in any other community.
Anything that comes out of those villages
has that particular power—
spiritual power.

You are born with that spirit but
it's up to you to feel responsible
to it and to develop it in a way
that you would be proud to say
''I'm a Hopi'' or ''I'm a Navajo.''
It's a tradition.
It's a language.
It's an identity.

Holy people have placed all of the gifts at the east.

Horses, cattle, sheep, children, old age,

medicine, songs, prayers—

placed all these things at the east.

Our hogan, she faces east.

The sun, as it comes over, penetrates into the home.

When we awake, we see that light. We know there is life.

Ceremony

We are all of one human life, human world.
We're also involved in the animal world,
and the plant world, and the cosmos.
And the simple teaching is that we are the ones who
would have to realize this and live in harmony with the earth
and all things that *move* on the earth.
It's a simple belief.
This is what makes the Hopi people strong.

I can call Talking God, Father Sky, Mother Earth,
First Man, First Woman,
Monster Slayer, Child Born of Water.
I can call them and they'll listen to me because the holy people
have given me these songs, this language, these ceremonies.

When a person died,
they would literally
burn everything that he had
that belonged to him.
His shoes, his clothes...

The rituals that we have are sacred.
And they're powerful.

Owls represent the spirits of people who have died.

When we die, we go to the east, we go to the light.
And it's a very powerful place to start from,
and a very powerful place to end.

We have a ceremony down there that we call Guyin.
It's a cleansing and blessing of the earth, the sky,
the animals, the mountains. Usually it starts out with a hunt.
In the late evening the singing begins.
And they sing about the wind and they sing about the clouds,
and how the clouds and the wind and the thunder
enact together to create the rain.
The land brings out the seed and it provides
the people, the Papago people, nourishment, strength.

The sun determines planting dates, time for the Niman ceremony,
which is the last kachina dance of the year.

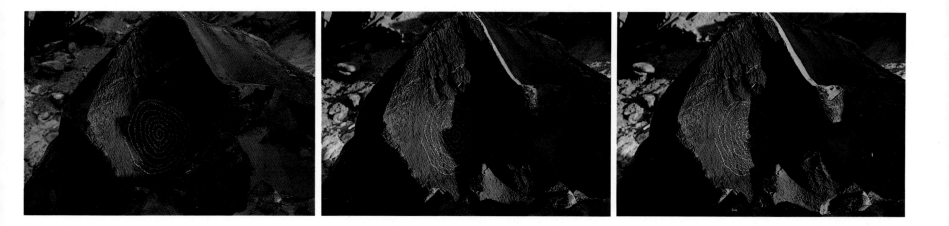

Kachina dolls were to educate the female youngsters.
When they possess these things which were given to them
by kachinas, they will learn how to care for them and then,
in turn, when they grow older,
they will learn how to take care of their people.

Every kachina doll has got a reason.
Each kachina has got a task.
Each has a reason for being made.
They relate to the universe, to the earth, to the plants,
to the insects, to the animals, to the waters.
Everything that is on this earth is represented by a kachina.
This is the way Hopi is.

Watch, be a part, see.

Through that you can come to an understanding.

For me, from a dance there's always a message, a teaching.

The real simple things, they add up to a lot.

Kachinas are intermediaries
between the Creator
and humankind.
The Creator delivers to us life
and health and happiness and hope
and faith
through the kachinas.
I can't think of too many words
to describe the feeling that I get
when I watch these dances.
I can say I'm inspired,
that I'm moved,
but it goes beyond that.

Artists

First, we're artists because we want to create.
Then, because I'm Indian,
I will reflect some of my Indianness
through these mediums.

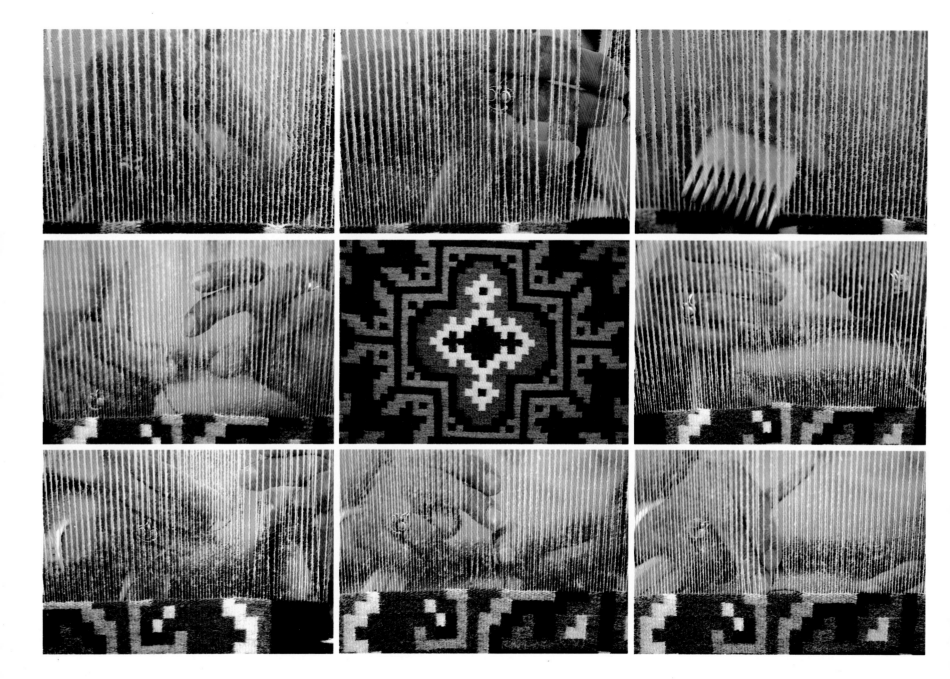

All these things were taught to me,
that weaving was a way of expressing yourself
rather than telling someone else what was going on inside of you.
I rarely tell anyone what is really in my rugs,
the feelings that I put into it.

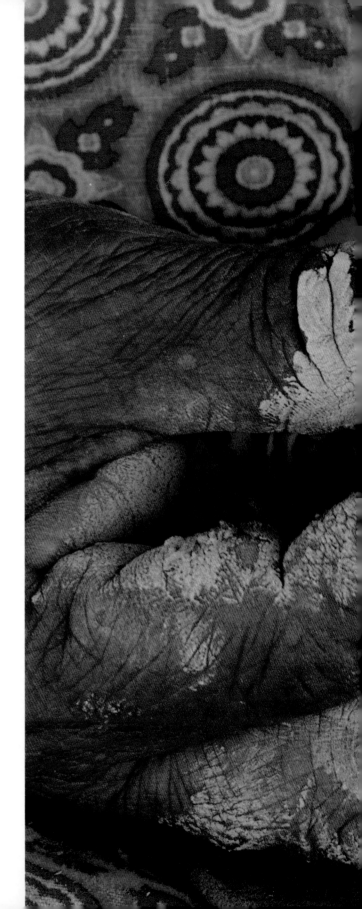

My grandmother
persuaded me to make pottery.
She was blind,
and she used to
feel my hand and feel my face,
and she told me
I was going to be a potter.
So . . . here I am!

114 ARTISTS

My pieces are traditional as they can be because they are from *me*.

I'm still learning about the Hopi culture, religion.
All of those experiences fall back to that piece of wood.
You'll be looking at the clouds one day and see a long-hair dancer.
The fluffy feathers coming out from the back
remind you of clouds coming up after a rainstorm.
You look at that wood and it's just there.

My great-grandfather and my grandfathers were shamans.
They sang wind songs and healing songs.
I use the wind as a power source to dry my masks.
I won't use a mask that's dried with a bad wind.
The good winds affect your attitude, affect your spirit,
your feelings. You let your mind rest and you feel the wind—
it either smothers you or releases your freedom.

My pieces start out somewhere deep down inside of me.
I feel that physically I just make what comes out of me spiritually.
The pieces seem to mold themselves. I never really mold them.

There's willows down there.
We have to go in the canyons, and it's hard to get.
When we make the baskets our hands hurt.
They do that long time, so we have to do that, too.
We don't do it just like they did, but we try.

In the arts there's a lot of things that can be accomplished.
The deeper you get into it, the more you learn.

I am hoping to do some things that will surprise *me*.
I live art. I think art.
I want my mind pure and clean and able to think creatively.

The art I see for the Indians is the spiritualness . . .
thanking the Creator for all that He's done.

Continuity

We have a traditional leader that has said that there will be
a time things will change so quickly it'll be just like a big dam
break loose and nobody's ever going to manage to stop it.
You will have different headdresses, you may even cut
your hair off and mingle up with the people with different tribes,
and you won't know which one is Hopi.

There will be roads up in the air.
You will be using boxes with wheels on.
These were the things that were prophesied in my younger days.
And I wondered, how it could be,
up in the air where the roads will be built?

And it's there. Today.
People up there, flying around like birds.

Today we are into a lot of things
that we claim is ours.
Land isn't ours.
Life isn't ours.
Language isn't ours.
Someone created that.

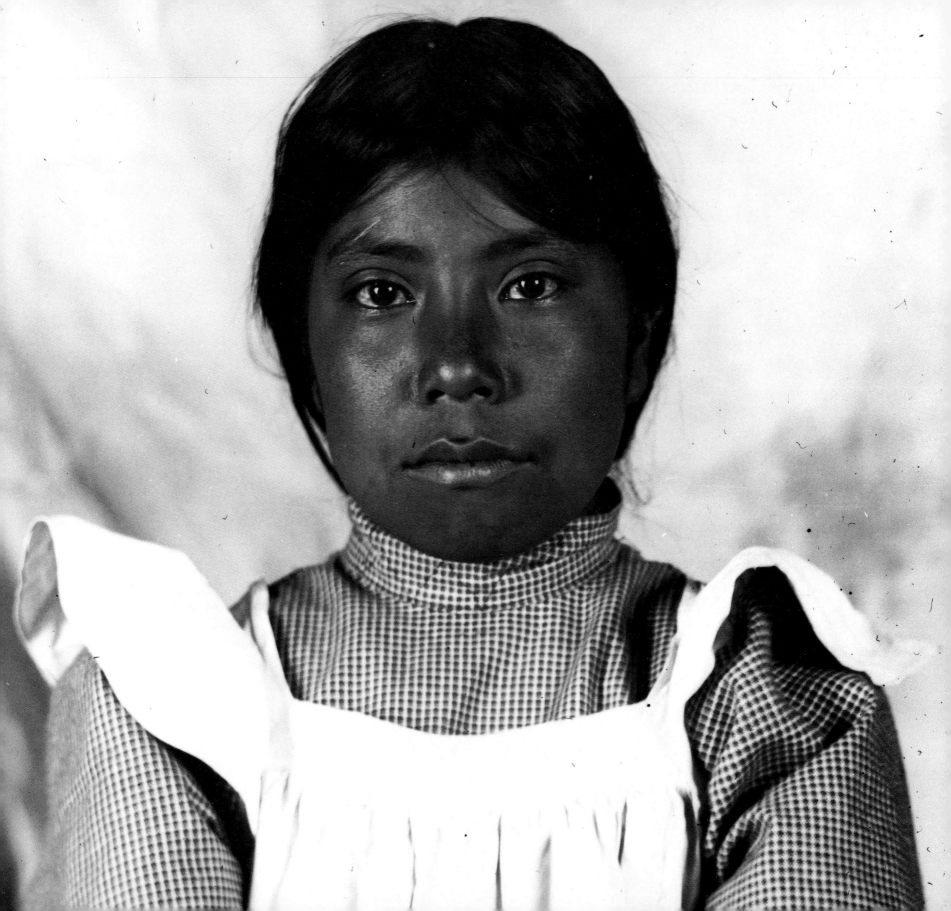

When we went to school, the interpreter told us,
"Forget your Hualapai language. Forget your Indian food.
Forget your stories.
Forget the names of the mountains and the rivers.
And above all, forget your language. Just speak English."

Nevertheless, we keep the principles of our tradition *in* our hearts.

It's something that brings a lot of
pride in people to be able to say,
"Here's something here
that belongs to me—
that's my language,
that's the way it's written,
this is what it means."

I had a hard time in school.

I wanted to learn how to rope and how to hunt.

I wanted to learn about the snakes and the lizards and the tortoises.

I remember sneaking out the window during class
and running off to the desert.

In time, I realized that I was involved in two different worlds.

I'd go out to the village and speak nothing but Papago.

And I enjoyed that.

That was me.

I was born knowing Hualapai and no English at all.
It was a problem. I had to think Indian, I had to think English.
In order to bring the two together, there was a pause.

I have a lot of trouble

trying to adjust to both worlds and trying to mix the two.

Whether I'm on the reservation

I cannot think the way I do in Flagstaff,

and I can't think the way I do on the reservation in Flagstaff.

That's just a totally different way of thinking.

You can't learn anything without giving something up.

I see a lot of creative people on the reservation.
They're caught in a paradoxical situation.
They adhere to the values
of what the grandmothers and grandfathers talked about,
to be in tune with themselves,
to be in tune with their environment.
But then when it comes to applying for a job,
then they don't have the degrees.

This value system that I'm telling you about goes this way,
and the other value system comes back the opposite way.
And I'm telling young Indian people that
there is a place there,
right down the middle.
Not too far to this side, not too far to that side,
but down the middle between pairs of opposites.

Creating "Our Voices, Our Land"

Somber dawn storm clouds trailed tendrils of rain down to the desert as I flew in a high-wing Cessna over Four Peaks in the Superstition mountain range near Phoenix. Somewhere below, in the vast reaches of the Southwest, Steve Trimble drove his rackety pickup truck over reservation roads; perhaps he was speaking with an elderly Indian woman who was recounting tales told by her grandmother: ". . . I see these things still in my own eyes yet. When, when, will I ever forget?" R. Carlos Nakai, Navajo/Ute Indian flutist and composer, worked on a musical score. Bonnie Durrance, at home in Washington, D.C., was editing the voices that Steve had already sent to her: ". . . out of these unstructured reminiscences, I began to compose a tone poem in seven stanzas in which the melody and cadence of the voice bore as much meaning as the words themselves. The voices became as solo instruments in an orchestra, each enhancing the other, adding resonance, building harmonies, forming a stream of consciousness, not only of individuals but of a people."

The pilot steadied the craft, and we leveled off. The red ball of the rising sun blazed between black peaks, and great shafts of light stabbed the desert floor. I pointed my motorized Nikon through the open window—the egg-shaped gyro-stabilizer attached to the camera spun at 20,000 rpm, acting as an invisible tripod. I squeezed the shutter gently and fired off sequences of three images each, which were ultimately joined to make panoramas of the dawn sky, the mountains, and the golden light.

Creating three-screen panoramas from a moving, unstable aircraft was an experiment, one that worked. These images now appear during the landscape interludes in "Our Voices, Our Land," the sound, image, and light show that sets the scene for the Heard's permanent exhibition, "Native Peoples of the Southwest."

I was photographing at Point Lobos, along the rugged California coastline a few miles south of Carmel, when I received a call from Ralph Appelbaum, whose New York design firm specializes in the creation of museum exhibits. Ralph asked if I would be interested in working on an audio-visual show for The Heard Museum. This phone call led to a year of joyful work with a group of gifted and talented artists as I

Afterword

149

became executive producer and director for the show that I entitled "Our Voices, Our Land."

This show became a living part of the new wing that houses "Native Peoples of the Southwest," an exhibition that *Washington Times* reporter Horst Bucholz described as "...likely to become the decade's most important exhibit of the Southwest Indian heritage."

During an early meeting with Ralph, Michael J. Fox (director of the museum), Dr. Robert G. Breunig (chief curator), and Pat Neary (Heard Museum designer), the critical question was posed: How can we create a new kind of museum experience, one that will enhance the collection, and one that will fulfill Michael Fox's desire: "We don't want to be just an institution that represents the native American people; we want to be an institution that participates *with* the native American people."

The consensus was that a three-screen show that portrayed seven thematic cycles of Indian culture—The Sun and the Land; Water, Rain, Subsistence; Architecture, Village, Community; The Family; Ceremony; Artists; Continuity— would best achieve this goal. Ideas were explored; Ralph conceived of a short show made up of the seven thematic cycles. I suggested that we expand the length of the show to thirty-seven minutes and use the seven themes as independent cycles of three minutes each. In the completed show that grew out of this plan,

voices of native Americans constitute the narration, accompanied by an original instrumental sound track. The theme cycles are separated by panoramic landscape interludes of one to two minutes each. These landscapes depict southwestern regions that are the tribe's historical and modern homelands. The interludes play to music only.

Finally, we added a series of lighting events, during which the spotlights illuminate artifacts of native American life. The screens go dark and the sound moves to spotlighted glass cases containing cradleboards, pottery, and kachina dolls.

My purpose in lengthening the show was to create a new kind of museum experience. "Our Voices, Our Land" has no beginning or end. Visitors could enter the show, leave it at any time to view the main exhibits, and return. Mike Fox courageously agreed to go ahead with this unique concept for a museum a/v show. The large body of images and words that grew out of the expanded version gave rise to this book.

Later, Ralph Appelbaum wrote a summary of our ideas: "...it would be a constant event. ...Visitors could see it upon entering or leaving. They could see the whole program...or view part of it.... The a/v experience was conceived as a decompression chamber for the busy tourist, tour group, student, or family.

"We want a space where one's contemporary sense of time could be slowed down as people encountered the time of the native American world. This is a time based on rural living, the sun, and the planting cycle. It is a time that is much slower, more introspective, and more visually concerned with the land . . . ."

We were on the verge of a new and perhaps revolutionary museum show. The theme cycles—the Indians' own voices, original native American music, sounds of nature, three-screen images, and panoramas and lighting events— were designed to reveal the inner life of the people.

The paramount agreement, however, was that our group *must not* interpose our ways, our culture, our prejudices between the native American and the visitors. We must view ourselves as crystal goblets and let *their* voices, *their* feelings and ideas, *their* culture and heritage shine through. As much as possible, we must not be visible at all.

After the meetings were finished, we divided the field work. Stephen Trimble would record extemporaneous talks with native Americans on the reservations and elsewhere and photograph these individuals during his sessions. My share was to photograph the three-screen panoramas of landscapes that would constitute the musical interludes, and to photograph the Indians themselves whenever possible. This required a number of trips to the Southwest from my New York City base; most important were the trips during the July and August thunderstorm periods. The eloquent light that bathes the land before and after the storms is a powerful inducement to any photographer.

I roamed the Indian lands, tracking thunderstorms and golden light and the crackling blue skies, filled with cloud castles, of the high plateaus. At Saguaro National Monument near Tucson, I photographed the giant cactus, and later picked sharp spines out of my legs. One sunset over Monument Valley, I opened the window of our Cessna and felt an icy blast of air, as Sentinel Mesa and the Mitten Buttes cast long shadows over the desert.

I witnessed dawns, dusks, and sunsets filled with magic: the Sangre de Cristos after a thunderstorm; the hush at Grand Canyon and on the Hopi reservation before dawn; the glow of dying light on the rocky fortress of Acoma Pueblo, "Sky City." One morning, I shared the silent beauty of the sunrise at Organ Pipe National Monument with a fledgling hawk perched on a nearby cactus.

My journeys criss-crossed Arizona and New Mexico. In Sedona, south of Flagstaff, shafts of light painted the rocks rusty orange, crimson, and mauve during a long sunset. The moon rose between tattered remnants of clouds in the slate-blue sky. Taos Pueblo blazed with great bonfires on Christmas eve; we alternately roasted and shivered as we inhaled thick smoke. A procession of Indians marched through the snow to the church, carrying burning logs and firing guns into the air. Another dawn found me on the overlook at Monument Valley Tribal Park; at least twenty cameras were aimed at the view and the freezing air snapped with German, French, Japanese, and the clicking of shutters.

In San Ildefonso Pueblo, near Santa Fe, I spent the day at an arts and crafts fair. Everyone seemed happy, and artists and dancers from many tribes cheerfully posed for me. I often remember the tiny children with painted faces and somber eyes, children who are now a permanent part of the museum's presentation.

I first encountered R. Carlos Nakai, education assistant at The Heard Museum, near the Lukachukai Mountains on the northwestern boundary of the vast Navajo Reservation. The Heard had sent him to guide me and my son, Andrei, around Navajo country for a few days. Carlos, I discovered, was a flute player, a music teacher, and a composer. Later, he invited me to his home in Phoenix to listen to his music. After hearing some of his compositions, melodies springing from native American themes, I decided to ask him to create the musical score for the show. Serendipitously, Robert Breunig had had this idea at the same time.

Carlos's perception of the assignment is revealing: "... the unifying element of these patterns is the harmolodic modulation of the Plains Indians' flutes and contemporary electronic instruments' variety of sounds. The flute melodies equivocate the ululations of anguished cries in supplication over our all-too-physical existence."

Bonnie Durrance, producer and associate director of the show, described her work in these words: "... In August, forty-five hours worth of disembodied voices began pouring into my headphones: old women dreaming of Geronimo, young men feeling about their place in the world today, mothers, weavers, potters, poets, and old men who remembered where all of them had come from....

"My task was to preserve the truth, spirit,

tone, rhythm and feeling of their message. . . . Technique was *never* allowed to call attention to itself. Images did not flicker, blink, flash or dance around the screens. They moved as if in a procession, meditatively, as the music would have it."

That October, with the show deadline almost upon us, I visited Bonnie at her home in Washington, D.C. There, she presided over a maze of four- and eight-track recorders, a computerized AVL Eagle multi-screen show programmer, nine projectors lit and humming, endless trays of slides, a light box covered with slides, and an almost impenetrable tangle of wires that meandered in every direction.

Her eyes gleamed as she invited me to watch a rough-cut of "Our Voices, Our Land." I stood with Steve and a few other friends amidst the chaos and watched. At the end, there was silence, then applause. The show was alive.

The finished show clearly demonstrates that the words of the native Americans are a kind of music. Passion and heartache, loneliness and anger and tenderness, love and reverence for the land, and a deep caring for one another and for the traditions that they cherish and fight to

keep alive: these profound and exquisitely human rhythms echo from the speakers. The voices often shake with emotion, and the spirit of the people lives on the soundtrack.

The score created by R. Carlos Nakai is a tender and often celebratory accompaniment to these voices. It sings of the land and the people, of sacred mountains and eternal deserts, of the clouds and the sky, and of the great spirits that live in those places. It *is* the Indian way.

Of the many journeys that I have made over the years across the landscapes of America, these visits hold a sacred place in my heart. It is my hope that the land remains unspoiled and holy for all generations. All of us who worked on this project, all who come to see and hear "Our Voices, Our Land," and wander through the exhibits in the new wing, and all who read this book have, I feel, a similar goal: that we may come to know and understand both the profound artistry in life and reverence for the land shown by the Indians, and the rich cultural heritage of their homes in the Southwest.

May I return again to walk in beauty.

HARVEY LLOYD

STEPHEN TRIMBLE has lived in the Southwest all of his life. Born in Denver, he received a liberal arts education from Colorado College and a master's degree in ecology from the University of Arizona. Trimble's writing and photography career grew from his work as a park ranger in

Utah and Colorado in the early 1970s, and his interpretive guides to national parks from North Dakota to California have won many awards.

His books include: *The Bright Edge: A Guide to the National Parks of the Colorado Plateau, Longs Peak: A Rocky Mountain Chronicle, Canyon Country* (with photographs by Dewitt Jones), and *Blessed By Light: Visions of the Colorado Plateau.* He has published photographs in *Audubon* Magazine and National Geographic Books, and has been a major contributor to *The Sierra Club Guides to the National Parks.*

In 1981, Trimble left his position as editor/publisher of the Museum of Northern Arizona Press, Flagstaff, to become a full-time free-lancer. In addition to being primary photographer and interviewer for "Our Voices, Our Land," his projects have included: editor, photographer, and writer for the Paul Winter Consort's Grand Canyon album, *Canyon;* primary photographer for the University of Nevada Press Great Basin Natural History Series; and author of the forthcoming biogeography volume in the series.

Trimble's current book projects include an introduction to contemporary Pueblo Indian pottery; editing and introducing an anthology of writings by literary naturalists; and a collection of reminiscences by old-timers in New Mexico. He lives near Santa Fe, New Mexico.

HARVEY LLOYD, internationally recognized location and aerial photographer, writer, and director, was born in New York City. His company, Image Makers, produces films and multi-screen shows.

In 1984, he directed, photographed for, and produced the three-screen sound, image, and light show "Our Voices, Our Land." The show runs continuously at the new wing on Native Peoples of the Southwest of The Heard Museum in Phoenix, Arizona.

Lloyd began his career working as a photo-journalist for *New York Magazine* and *The Saturday Evening Post.* Since then he has traveled over three-quarters of a million miles for magazine, multi-screen, film, and advertising clients.

His large format picture book, *Voyages of the Royal Vikings,* photographed from the air, sea, and land at ports-of-call around the world, received the *Communication Arts* 1985 Design Annual's Award of Excellence.

Lloyd has received numerous other awards for his films and photography, and has appeared on the Nikon television series, "The Photographer's Eye," in a half-hour show of his works.

A past president of the American Society of Magazine Photographers (ASMP), he is currently chairman of the society's Awards Committee. Lloyd teaches master classes at the Maine Photographic Workshops.

His shows and screenings include The Museum of Modern Art, New York, The Grand Palais Museum, Paris, The International Center of Photography, New York, The Arles International Photography Festival, The United Nations, and the United States Bicentennial.

Lloyd's current projects include a book of his aerial photographs. When not on the road somewhere in the world, he lives in Manhattan.

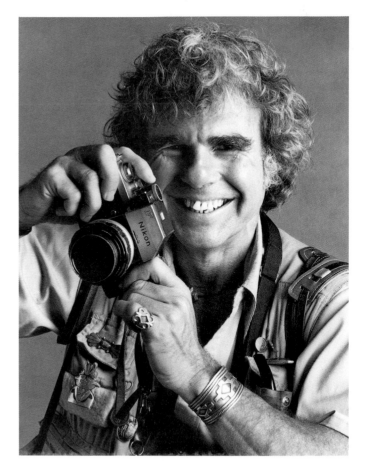

Technical Notes

All of the photography for *Our Voices, Our Land* was made using Nikon F3 cameras and Kodachrome ASA 25 and ASA 64 film.

Harvey Lloyd:

I work with five cameras with motor drives and an assortment of fixed-focus and zoom lenses. The lenses range from 15 mm super-wide-angle to 300 and 500 mm telephotos. While I use all of my lenses for shooting, I prefer the 85 mm and the 105 mm for closeup portraits.

I prefer fixed-focus lenses. They are generally sharper, easier to focus, and much faster than zooms. I rarely use any filters other than skylights and polarizers to deepen the skies.

In the desert landscapes, with their harsh light and extremes of contrast, I bracket a lot, often two, three, and four f-stops up and down. The best light is found during the "magic" hours of dawn and sunset, and before and after thunderstorms.

My assistants and I always arise before dawn during a shoot, and we photograph until after sunset. In the summer, such days may run eighteen hours, and they are thoroughly enjoyed, at least by me.

I photograph every subject from a variety of distances and angles, seeking the best composition. I am very careful to see what the *camera sees,* and I do not believe in cropping my pictures after they are taken.

I do aerial photography from fixed-wing airplanes and helicopters, removing the door from the helicopters (and light planes, when possible). I gaffer-tape my seat buckle for security.

When shooting in the air, I always use a Ken Lab gyro-stabilizer, a small black "egg" that spins at 20,000 rpm and attaches to the tripod mount of my Nikons. The gyro absorbs vibration and helps me create sharp images.

To create the three-screen, three-image panoramas seen in "Our Voices, Our Land," I used a ball head on my Gitzo tripod. The ball head enables me to selectively "eyeball" the composition of the panoramas, which I prefer to the fixed level vision of a panoramic head on the tripod. For aerial panoramas, I use the gyro-stabilizer and pray.

When photographing native Americans, or anyone, I am extremely polite. I smile and ask permission, sometimes with just a nod of my

The Speakers and the Photographs

head as I raise my camera. I never photograph unless the subject agrees. It often helps to have a local person act as a guide and friend on Indian lands and in other unfamiliar situations and locations.

I love photography and I am never happier than when on location in the United States or anywhere in the world.

Stephen Trimble:

I work with two cameras, now F3's, and in my earlier days, Nikkormats. My lenses range from 20 mm to 500 mm. I use an 80–200 mm zoom constantly, for portraits and for middle-distance landscapes. I use a motor drive, and sometimes the automatic exposure setting, for fast-moving subjects like rodeos and ceremonial dances.

I prefer Kodachrome 25 but use Kodachrome 64 when I feel I must. I underexpose both films slightly to achieve more saturated color. I use a tripod and cable release virtually all of the time. For landscapes, I usually want maximum depth of field, which often requires shutter speeds of 1/8 second when I am shooting slow (but wonderful) Kodachrome 25. Only the tripod makes this possible. The tripod not only ensures sharp pictures, but allows me

to maintain eye contact with my portrait subjects after I have set up the shot. My Gitzo tripod is solid, compact, and indestructible.

I made many of the portraits in *Our Voices, Our Land* in open shade behind buildings and under trees, in the few moments when a passing cloud created "studio light" for me, or on stormy days. In the full summer sunlight between about 8:00 A.M. and 5:00 P.M., landscape photography is well nigh impossible.

In trying to communicate the power of these faces, I made my compositions very tight, moving in on eyes and expressions. This is risky: frame a tiny bit too tightly and the person looks awkward, their head unsettlingly chopped off. But when it works, the subject looks right out at you from the screen or the page with great force, and the viewer is not aware of my violation of the rule: "never cut off anyone's head."

At ceremonies, I try to be attentive, respectful, invisible, and ever-sensitive to when photography is inappropriate. I try to live up to the advice of Ernst Haas: "The more you are able to forget your equipment, the more time you have to concentrate on the subject and on the composition. The camera should become an extension of your eye, nothing else."

Captions:

Note: In each instance, the source of the photograph is given; the initials (ST/Stephen Trimble, HL/Harvey Lloyd) indicate the appropriate photographer.

page x: *Top row*—Hualapai memorial mourning ceremony, Peach Springs, Arizona (left and center); Papago woman, Topawa, Arizona (right). *Middle row*—Pima basket dancers, Sacaton, Arizona. *Bottom row*—singer, Apache girl's puberty ceremony, Whiteriver, Arizona (left); Hualapai elder, Peach Springs, Arizona (center); Hualapai man, Peach Springs, Arizona (right). ST

page 4: Laguna Pueblo, New Mexico. ST

page 7: Pueblo girl, New Mexico. HL

page 8: San Francisco Peaks, Arizona. ST

page 9: Red Rock Country, Sedona, Arizona. HL

page 10: Monument Valley, Arizona. HL aerial

page 11: words—Hualapai man.

pages 12–13: words—male Hopi elder; photo: rainbow, Pojoaque Valley, New Mexico. ST

page 14: words—Hualapai man; photos: storm, Rio Grande Valley, New Mexico. HL

page 15: words—Hualapai man; photos: Sandia Mountains, New Mexico. HL

pages 16–17: words—Hualapai man; photo: Monument Valley, Arizona. HL

page 18: Gila River, San Carlos Apache Reservation, Arizona. ST

page 19: words—Papago man; photo: sunset, Courthouse Butte, Sedona, Arizona. ST

page 20–21: words—Hualapai man; photo: Baboquivari Peak, Arizona. ST aerial

page 22: moonset/sunrise, Vermilion Cliffs, Arizona. ST

page 23: words—Papago man.

page 24: words—Hopi woman; photos: Organ Pipe Cactus National Monument, Arizona. HL

page 25: Monument Valley, Arizona. HL

page 26: San Francisco Peaks from Mogollon Rim, Arizona. ST

page 27: words—Navajo man; photos: San Francisco Peaks, Arizona. HL

page 28: saguaro cactus, Arizona. HL

page 29: aspen leaves, southern Utah (left); lupine, San Francisco Peaks, Arizona (center); beavertail cactus blossom, Sonoran Desert (right). ST

page 30: mud cracks, Colorado River, southern Utah. ST

page 31: words—Hopi man; photos: moon and Joshua Tree, Grand Wash Cliffs, Arizona (left); south from Picacho Peak, Arizona (center); moonset/sunrise, Saguaro National Monument, Arizona (right). ST

pages 32–33: words—male Hopi elder; photo: lightning, southern Utah. ST

pages 34–35: words—Papago man; photo: saguaro fruits, Saguaro National Monument, Arizona. ST

page 36: Havasu Falls, Arizona. ST

page 37: words—female Hualapai elder; photos: native pumpkin, Rio Grande Valley, New Mexico. ST

page 38: words—Hopi man; photos: Eagle Clan corn field, Hopi Reservation, Arizona. ST

page 39: Hopi corn, Arizona. ST

page 40: words—Hopi woman.

page 41: Hopi woman grinding corn; photo by Victor Masayesva, Jr.

page 42: words—Hualapai man (above); Navajo man (below).

page 43: mule deer, southern Utah. ST

page 44: words—female Hualapai elder; photos: agave, Mogollon Rim, Arizona (left); cattails, Colorado (center); mesquite beans, Avra Valley, Arizona (right). ST

page 45: words—female Hualapai elder; photos: saguaro cactus, Arizona. HL

page 46: thundercloud over Truchas Peak, Sangre de Cristo Range, New Mexico. ST

page 47: words—Hualapai man; photos: Roosevelt Lake, Arizona. HL aerial

page 48: Pueblo man and child, New Mexico. HL

page 49: Navajo family, Red Mesa, Utah (left); Papago couple, Arizona (center); Apache baby, Whiteriver, Arizona (right). ST

page 50: young Hualapai woman and baby, Peach Springs, Arizona. ST

page 51: words—Hualapai man; photo: medicine man healing, Apache girl's puberty ceremony, Whiteriver, Arizona. ST

page 52: Navajo bead-seller, Little Colorado Gorge Overlook, Arizona. ST

page 53: words—Navajo man; photos: Navajo family hogans, Red Mesa, Utah. ST

page 54: young Hualapai woman, Peach Springs, Arizona. ST

page 55: words—Hopi woman; photos: Papago women, Arizona. ST

pages 56–59: words—Apache medicine man; photos: Apache girl's puberty ceremony, Whiteriver, Arizona. ST

pages 60–61: words—Hopi woman; photos: Hopi hair dressing, courtesy Southwest Museum, Los Angeles, California. Neg. Nos. 20,379; 20,380; 22,577; 20,381 (left to right).

pages 62–63: words: Hopi woman; photo: Hopi boy, Polacca, Arizona. ST

page 64: words—Apache medicine man.

page 65: Fannie and Lorenzo, Havasupai, courtesy Department Library Services, American Museum of Natural History, Neg. No. 316864.

pages 66–67: words—Navajo woman; photo: Hualapai girl, Arizona. ST

page 68: Walpi, Hopi Mesas, photo by George Alexander Grant, courtesy National Park Service.

page 69: Santo Domingo Pueblo, courtesy Arizona State Museum, University of Arizona, photographer: Forman Hanna (left); Zuni Pueblo, courtesy Southwest Museum, Los Angeles, California. Neg. No. 24,059 (center); Zuni Pueblo, National Anthropological Archives, Smithsonian Institution, Photo No. 2267-i (right).

page 70: words—Hualapai man.

page 71: Zuni man, courtesy Western History Collection, Natural History Museum of Los Angeles County.

page 72: words—female Hualapai elder.

page 73: Pima woman, courtesy National Anthropological Archives, Smithsonian Institution, Photo No. 4533.

page 74: San Juan Pueblo, New Mexico. ST

page 75: words—young Mojave/Navajo man; photos: Yavapai camp, courtesy National Anthropological Archives, Smithsonian Institution, Photo No. 76-5680 (left); Apache camp, courtesy Arizona Historical Society (center); Navajo hogan, courtesy Western History Collection, Natural History Museum of Los Angeles County (right).

page 76: words—Hualapai woman; photos: Montezuma Castle National Monument, Arizona (left); Twin Towers Ruin, Hovenweep National Monument, Utah (center); Pueblo Bonito, Chaco Culture National Historic Park, New Mexico (right). ST

page 77: moonrise, Casa Grande Ruins National Monument, Arizona. ST

pages 78–79: words—male Hopi elder; photo: Zuni living room, courtesy Western History Collection, Natural History Museum of Los Angeles County.

pages 80–81: words—Santa Clara Pueblo woman; photos: Taos Pueblo, New Mexico. HL

pages 82–83: words—Hopi man; photo: Hopi woman grinding corn, courtesy Field Museum of Natural History, Chicago.

page 84: prayer feathers in fir tree, San Juan Pueblo deer dance, New Mexico. ST

page 85: words—Navajo man; photos: Second Mesa, Hopi Reservation, Arizona. HL

page 86: ogre kachinas at kiva, Hopi Mesas, courtesy Jo Mora Collection, Northern Arizona University Library.

page 87: Yuma man, courtesy Arizona State Museum, University of Arizona, photographer: Taber Portrait Studio (left); Pima man, courtesy National Anthropological Archives, Smithsonian Institution, Photo No. 2693-A (center); Navajo man, courtesy Western History Collection, Natural History Museum of Los Angeles County (right).

page 88: deer dance, San Juan Pueblo, New Mexico. ST

page 89: words— Hopi man; photos: rock art, Zuni Reservation, New Mexico (left and center); singer, Hualapai mourning ceremony, Peach Springs, Arizona (right). ST

page 90: Yei dancer, courtesy The Heard Museum.

page 91: words—Navajo man.

pages 92–93: words—Hualapai man; photo: Hualapai mourning ceremony, Peach Springs, Arizona, ST

pages 94–95: words—Hopi woman; photo: Turtle dance, Taos Pueblo, New Mexico, courtesy The Heard Museum.

page 96: words—Papago man; photos: cemetery, San Xavier Mission, Arizona. ST

page 97: words—Papago man; photos: saguaro cacti, Arizona. HL

page 98: Niman dance, Hopi Mesas, courtesy National Anthropological Archives, Smithsonian Institution, Photo No. 79-4289.

page 99: words—Hopi man; photos: petroglyph, prehistoric summer solstice marker, Petrified Forest National Park, Arizona. ST

page 100: words—Hopi man

page 101: Hopi girls with kachina dolls, Museum of Northern Arizona.

page 102: macaw feathers for sale, Santa Clara Pueblo feast day, New Mexico. ST

page 103: words—Apache man; photos: Tewa Pueblo comanche dancers, New Mexico. (left and center, ST; right, HL)

pages 104–105: words—Hopi man; photo: Zuni longhair dancers, courtesy Western History Collection, Natural History Museum of Los Angeles County.

page 106: Navajo Yei rug. ST

page 107: Apache sculptor's studio, Cerrillos, New Mexico. ST

page 108: Hopi man spinning, courtesy Jo Mora Collection, Northern Arizona University Library.

page 109: words—young Jemez Pueblo woman; photos: Hopi woman weaving wicker plaque, courtesy Arizona State Museum, University of Arizona, photographer: Forman Hanna (left); Isleta Pueblo potter, courtesy The Heard Museum (center); Navajo weaver, courtesy The Heard Museum (right).

page 110: Navajo weaver and rug, Indian Market, Santa Fe, New Mexico. ST

page 111: words—Navajo woman.

pages 112–113: words—San Ildefonso Pueblo woman; photo: Hopi potter, Polacca, Arizona. ST

page 114: Navajo silversmith, courtesy Southwest Museum, Los Angeles, California. Neg. No. 20,722.

page 115: words—Navajo woman; photo: Apache basket weaver, courtesy The Heard Museum.

page 116: words—Hopi man; photos: Hopi kachina carver, Kykotsmovi, Arizona. ST

page 148: aerial sunrise, Four Peaks, Arizona (top row); Grand Canyon, Arizona (middle row); Acoma Pueblo, New Mexico (bottom row). HL

page 152: theater in which "Our Voices, Our Land" runs throughout the day at The Heard Museum; photo by A. F. Payne Photographic, Phoenix, Arizona.

page 156: *Top row*—cloud (left) HL; mule deer, southern Colorado (center) ST; Pueblo potter, New Mexico (right) HL. *Middle row*—rainbow, aerial, Navajo Reservation, Arizona (left) HL; princess, White Mountain Apache Tribal Fair, Arizona (center) ST; Enchanted Mesa, Acoma, New Mexico (right) HL. *Bottom row*—Laguna Pueblo mission church, New Mexico (left) ST; feast day, San Juan Pueblo, New Mexico (center) ST; San Xavier mission, Arizona (right). ST

HARVEY LLOYD: My deepest thanks to Michael Fox for his faith in me, for his endless encouragement, and for his understanding of the new kind of show that we were inventing and creating for The Heard Museum. That faith, in the end, made this book possible. I share heartily with Stephen Trimble in thanking the many workers on "Our Voices, Our Land," all of whom were dedicated beyond measure to the realization of our vision. Finally, and most importantly, I thank the true creators of the show, the native American peoples of the Southwest.

STEPHEN TRIMBLE: I thank Robert Breunig, for believing that I could carry out his vision for this show. His trust was a gift that transformed my career. I also thank my partners in "Our Voices, Our Land": Harvey Lloyd, for his directorial skill and his desire to see the show produced with uncompromised quality; Bonnie Durrance, for her creativity, intelligence, understanding, and grace under pressure; Michael Fox, for his unfailing support; R. Carlos Nakai, for his lyrical music; and Ralph Appelbaum, Gloria Caprio, and Pat Neary for clear vision and elegance in design. Mary Graham, The Heard Museum's librarian, gave crucial help with historic photos; her efficiency was a delight.

Mickey Houlihan of Wind Over the Earth Records, Boulder, Colorado, gave me a crash course in location sound recording and recommended our equipment. The staff of the Coconino Center for the Arts, Flagstaff, was generous in allowing use of their auditorium as a recording studio.

Karen and Gary Nabhan, Nick Bleser and Roberta Stabel, Karen and Bob Breunig, Jennifer Dewey, Kathryn Wilde, Deedy Young, and most especially Susan Shaffer and Victor Nahmias gave me moral support, creative logistical assistance, and generally took care of me while on the road. Many people recommended voices and faces to us. Particular thanks go to Eugene Sekaquaptewa and Joann Fischer, Kykotsmovi, Arizona; and Bruce Hucko, Montezuma Creek, Utah.

The show would never have become a book without the determination of Gary Avey at The Heard Museum and Bruce Andresen and Susan McDonald of Northland Press. I am grateful to them for their commitment to the project. I also thank my partner in design, David Jenney, for his dedication, cooperation, and good taste.

Most of all, I thank the many Indian people whose generosity in sharing their lives enriches us all. Lucille Watahomigie and Malinda Powskey, Peach Springs, Arizona, deserve special recognition. I also wish to acknowledge the inspiration of the late Philip Cassadore, Peridot, Arizona, and the late Percy Lomaquahu, Hotevilla, Arizona. I hope this book does honor to their spirits.

Acknowledgments

DESIGNED BY
STEPHEN TRIMBLE AND DAVID JENNEY
COMPOSED IN PHOTOTYPE GARAMOND
BY PREPRESS GRAPHICS, FLAGSTAFF, ARIZONA
PRINTED ON QUINTESSENCE GLOSS
BY TOPPAN PRINTING COMPANY, JAPAN
PUBLISHED BY

NORTHLAND PRESS
FLAGSTAFF, ARIZONA